I0169262

you think I'm serious, but I'm joking

Georgia Tell

Copyright © 2018 by Georgia Tell

This is a work of fiction. The characters and events described herein are imaginary and are not intended to refer to specific places or to living persons alive or dead. All rights reserved. No part of this publication may be reproduced, distributed, or transmitted in any form or by any means, including photocopying, recording, or other electronic or mechanical methods without the prior written permission of the publisher except for brief quotations embodied in critical reviews.

ISBN 978-0-9995788-4-1

Published by Blue Hair Books

Visit author's website: www.GeorgiaTell.com
Follow author on Twitter and Instagram: @GeorgiaTell

Contents

Part 1
Public

The Life of Thomas Nowak

When he is in the womb, Thomas doesn't realize it.
He hears the big slow noises, and that's all he
  knows.
His birth is uneventful.
The doctor, his father and his big sister Jackie
  greet him with more enthusiasm than he's
  prepared for.
He cries.

He is good baby and a good toddler.
His parents' neighbor, a childless and widowed
  Mrs. Brook, watches him.
Twice, she contemplates taking him and running
  away, but she grabs her keys and Thomas
  giggles at the sound.
Her body relaxes, and she smiles and waits for Mr.
  Nowak.

His first word is "Wommy."
His mother squeals with delight and brags to her
  husband.
Little do they know, he is trying to say "Tommy."
He learns "Mommy," "Papa," and "Wackie," much
  to his big sister's chagrin.
She tells all her friends at school the next day that
  he said "Jackie."

First day of kindergarten, he lets go of his
  Mommy's hand and strides forward.

He dresses up as Batman for Halloween, gets a
    mancala game for Christmas, and is the
    sidekick in the kindergarten play.

When he is fourteen, he falls in love with a girl
    named Rebecca.
She has red hair and freckles.
She holds his hand twice when they sit in front of
    school waiting to be picked up.
He picks dandelions for her.
His body feels alive.
He thinks about her in every spare moment.
He kisses her once.
Jared Werthing asks her to homecoming.
She says yes.
Thomas says he's happy for her, but when he gets
    home, he shoves his head into a pillow and
    breathes raggedly for the rest of the night.

During senior year, Thomas asks a girl in his math
    class to prom.
She says yes.
She hangs out with her friends the whole time,
    because Thomas can only look at Rebecca and
    Jared dancing.

Thomas leaves Fresno at his first chance.
He goes to NYU.
He doesn't do well his first semester.
Or the second semester.

His father calls him and says that they can't pay for
    his education if he doesn't take it seriously.
Thomas gets drunk three nights a week.
Thursday night, Friday night, and Saturday night.
He speaks to his advisor.
Ms. Frenk tells him that the only major he can do
    and graduate on time is English.
He cuts the drinking down to two nights a week
    and studies more.
Rebecca crosses his mind sometimes, but he
    pushes her fuzzy red image out of his mind.
First semester of senior year, he takes
    Contemporary American Literature and
    decides he wants to write his thesis on a poet
    who drank himself to death.
Only his professor reads the thesis.
The professor gives him passing marks.
Thomas graduates.

His family travels to New York City for his
    graduation.
They ask about his plans.
Thomas deflects, because he doesn't have any.

Three weeks after graduation, Thomas gets offered
    a TA position in the English department.
He can take one free class a semester and gets a
    small stipend.

He dates three girls after graduation.

He gets exclusive with the third.
Her name is Rockelle.
She has red hair and freckles.
She reminds him of Rebecca.

They move in together quickly.
New York City is expensive.
They have sex often.
Rockelle is vivacious, and her friends don't know
what she sees in him, with his quiet demeanor
and slow way.
She fiercely loves him, and Thomas likes the
feeling.
He loves her too.

They marry in the fifth year of him TAing.

When Rockelle gets pregnant, Thomas notifies his
boss he will only stay through to the end of the
school year.

He gets a job as a copy editor.
He's good at it.

His first and only son is born.
Thomas's body feels alive.
He knows this is the best moment of his life.
They name their son Brendan.
He thinks about Brendan in every spare moment.

After three years, Thomas makes manager.
He's not as good at this.
They don't promote him again.
He gets cost of living adjustments every two years.

Brendan grows to be a lively and inquisitive boy,
    like his mother.
He's popular at school.
He plays junior varsity soccer in tenth grade and
    varsity during junior and senior years.
Thomas takes so many pictures.
Brendan goes to college in Los Angeles.
Thomas keeps his face strong.

Thomas works.
Rockelle works.
They're professionals now.
They dance in the kitchen together, singing Red
    Hot Chili Pepper songs, feeling like old people.

Thomas wonders where Rebecca is.
If she's with Jared.

At age 65, Thomas's supervisor hints that it's
    getting time to retire.
Thomas has nothing else to do.
He likes his work, though every other employee is
    at least ten years younger than him.
He forms a special relationship with the coffee
    maker.

Rockelle retires and visits their son who now lives in San Francisco.
She comes back with her face glowing.

Thomas's parents die in a car crash.
He sees his sister and his son at the funeral in Fresno.
The sky is bright blue.

His son is a father now with two daughters of his own.
Thomas loves seeing them.
They call him Crazy Grandpa because of all the faces he makes.
He buys them presents every time he sees them.
He brags about them when he goes back to work.

When Thomas is 67, his supervisor changes his job description to something Thomas can't do.
One month later, they have his retirement party.
There's a cake and two balloons.
One of his team members, John, tells a story about how Thomas helped him every night when he first started.
John is taking his place.

Rockelle and Thomas sell their small condo in New York City.
They move to San Francisco.

Thomas sees his grandchildren everyday, and he's
 happy.

He dies before Rockelle.
She's holding his hand, and his son is stuck in
 traffic.
His heart beats for the last time.
He thinks of Rebecca.
He frowns.

trich

he looked tan and sad
coming back from Miami
his wife didn't smile either
no one asked why
but he left soon after
an empty bottle of metronidazole
in his desk's wastebasket
an old diamond ring
in his desk's drawer
a paper slip with "Sorry."
on the desktop

$79.95

satin and sleek
a zipper in the back
she stares at the dress
stomach yearning
for the chance
to feel beautiful,
to feel rich
just once

she has no money
nickel wedged in the corner of her
ugly hand-me-down wallet
she asks her dad: You gotta earn
your own money.
That's what jobs are for.
Qualifications: Bachelor's degree
she looks online
she reads articles
she calls a survey company
"Nothing right now, I'll call you."
submit. submit. submit.

Sale Price: $79.95
she checks the dress online

Submit.

she walks
palms sweating in the Florida heat
but to be pretty,

she must do ugly things
a *free* ride, a blouse
4-year-old shoes too tight for her feet
she sits across the car's center console
from a man
hook nose and crisp white shirt

she frowns
Smile,
I'll throw in a tip.
she smiles
fumbling in the back of his car
she wipes
between her legs with the
starchy linen of her blouse

cash in hand:
$101

she goes home
blouse buried
in the bottom of the hamper
she showers
the stink of him
makes her gag
she feels ugly
she checks the dress online
Out of stock.
Uglier.

arbitrary

amidst stacks of hastily organized paper
along a non-descript wall with a clock on it
a small creaky desk with a nameplate
Him in the metal chair, rolled His eyes
He slowly stamped in red ink "DECEASED"
onto papers with pictures, names and life stories
His hand slipped but still came down on the paper
getting a splotch of red ink on a child's paper
He did not give the mistake a second thought
in Pennsylvania, a ten year old boy developed
      asthma
He continued to stamp rigorously
the done pile filled out and He smiled to Himself
"quitting time soon," He thought
billions of lives were put on hold for it
but before He left the office for the day
seven blue outlined papers were stamped
the metallic blue stamp said "MIRACLE"
He sighed and haphazardly cleared the desk

Part 2
Private

those tiny dangerous inklings in your gut
you get about a person are probably
accurate

"turn around, little bird"
says the gardener
little bird turns and chirps
the gardener smiles and squawks,
"you are so beautiful, little bird"
little bird flutters away in a hurry

getting to the top

the secretary looks down
at the beetle near her shoe
"will he promote me?" she asks
the beetle does not have a voice
she smashes the beetle

pruning is supposed to encourage growth

the gardener lops off a flower
he cuts off another and another
until the plant is bare
then he puts down his snippers
and walks inside into the house

can I be the tree?

let the wild tree be
unpruned for all to see
let the green branches be
naive and put out many leaves
let the bright blossoms be
free to grow fruits heavy
let the wild tree be
eager to live honestly

oh shit, never mind

the gardener pulled back the shower curtain
neatly trimmed beard and dirt-caked hands
stared at me under the water then
"get rid of the deadweight," said the man
but I cannot comply with the demand
a pair of pruners from his waistband
dull metal pushes on the index of my right hand
scream but there is no waking again

giving up for the fifth time that day

electrician crawls under the house
sand dirties his messy uniform
halfway through his job
he collapses and rests his head
among the dirt and cobwebs
he sleeps like he never has

painting

a thin-legged spider traipsed across
her newly painted wall
seemingly unaware of the work
she asked him why he was there
on her newly painted wall
he said, "I still need to get home"
so she smashed him
and got paint on her hand
and ruined her newly painted wall
but on her own terms

eavesdropping on man demanding self-mutilation as proof of love with lines from *Letter from Birmingham Jail* by Martin Luther King Jr.

I.
in the dark cherrywood dining room
the husband spins his argument
he has read the greats
"direct action seeks to create such a crisis"
"foster such a tension"
"it can no longer be ignored"
he needs her to prove that she loves him
he dissolves her will over days
nonstop
shadows cover his face

II.
artificial light of kitchen fluorescents engulfs the
        wife
she stands in the doorless doorway
three nights of no sleep
drag her face to the floor
her voice shakes more than her hands
she says:
okay, you can do it
"freedom is never voluntarily given"
clearly, the wife has never read Martin Luther King
        Jr.
she should know better

III.
the wicker chair scratches at my numb legs
the weighty book presses into my body
I'm reading *Letter from Birmingham Jail*
listening, I realize the words of great men depend
 entirely on context
I can't move under the heavy of the owl's words
"wait has almost always meant never"
I clip my own wings
not moving to intervene, pretending to not exist
flying is a feat best undertaken by the brave
and sharp edges of well-written words prove that
 logic is not kind
would I rather be a hummingbird or an owl?
unequivocally, I prefer nectar

IV.
the husband does not budge from his stance:
"lukewarm acceptance is much more bewildering
 than outright rejection"
anything less than her fingers is room
 temperature
she rattles around the disheveled kitchen drawer
her voice is pitchy:
you'll have to do it for me
she hasn't the stomach to cut off her own finger
neither do I
metal on her pinky; a sharp intake of breath before
 she says, *go*, with her eyes squeezed shut

his relief is the most sinister. I have witnessed it
    before when I made sacrifices
I wish to vomit, chunks of old pizza and acid
    dissolving the metal of the knife
he says:
all I wanted was for you to be willing
she surrendered
she keeps her finger
I smack into the window
I break my neck

Part 3
Where the fuck are we?

no bigs

some days you want to cut off your own fingers
take a sharp knife and slice 'em off like Play-Doh

it's not me

the world woke up weird
narrowly missed accidents
too much noise
my stomach hurts
can I be back home yet?

isaac and the knife

isaac did not fight
he stared up at his father and his Father
the glint of the knife on the mountain top
it blinded him
ropes were not necessary

isaac did not exist
the knife stared at him
the delusion of a willing victim
that dulled the knife
sacrifice was not necessary

giving up childhood dreams

when he was little
he locked the bathroom door
he had his mom's tension belts
long wide strips of elastic
and he watched himself
wrap them around his upper torso
he imagined leaving the bathroom
but he never did

small and strong and smashed

crush me
suddenly from above
I'm an ant
small and strong
smashed into the pavement

I can't just get over it and you can't talk

3 hens settle in for the night
clicking and clacking the day's gossip
rooster cried all morning about chicks
horse tripped in the mountain's ride
spider's web was ruined after a day's work
the hens clucked raucously, pitying the folly
but, they hadn't done anything that day

a geometric kaleidoscope of sad / sad poem

she told me she doesn't like sad poems
no more bugs being squashed
no more fingers cut off
no more dying in a bathtub
no more cars hitting bodies
no more falling off the roof
no more existential dread
no more staring out the window at rain
no more girls selling themselves for dresses
no more sarcasm about hoping to die
no more dripping wax onto my palm
no more boys counting the moments after death
no more wishing to be ripped away by disgusting
    hands
no more me

you think I'm joking, but I'm serious

I say I want to die
a lot
but I say it with a smile
and then I laugh
because I don't want to lie
but I don't want you to worry

disappearing is my goal
but I want to do it
with so much class
and so much grace
that you say,
"that chick's alright"

I want to disintegrate in a ballroom
wearing a gown of ice and pearls
waltzing across the polished oak wood
I am svelte

it must be without warning
I must be beautiful
then maybe
maybe I can start over

garden grows over the wall

She never gives me a knife
never asks for my devotion

but my Play-Doh hands are clasped
wildly chanting my obsession for Her nectar

giving every ounce of Herself
no need for proof of my love

Eve and Adam can't see Her
they think She is my delusion

but my garden overflows with Her touch
the shears buried deep under bedrock

About the Author

Georgia Tell lives in a house full of animals: cats, dogs, lizards, rats and fish. When she's not writing books, she loves to knit, crochet, and create many elaborate financial spreadsheets.

If Georgia could have any wish granted, she'd wish to know what happens forever: the history of the universe -- past, present and future.

www.GeorgiaTell.com
Twitter & Instagram: @GeorgiaTell

www.ingramcontent.com/pod-product-compliance
Lightning Source LLC
Chambersburg PA
CBHW031635040426
42452CB00007B/838